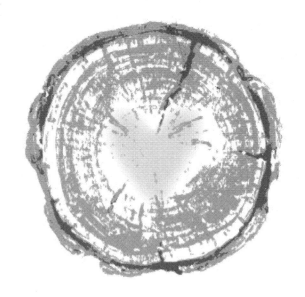

reclaimed

MAKING WHOLE WHAT
WAS BROKEN & BETRAYED

Small Group Study Guide

Stephanie Broersma

Practical Suggestions For Moving Through Grief

Through the sharing of her experiences following her husband's confession, Stephanie provides other women a companion in their own unique journey as they navigate the confusing and complex emotions surrounding infidelity. You will feel understanding as she walks with you, helping you navigate through the aftermath of unplanned pain and unending questions.

Stephanie's candid story of grief, turmoil and finding blessings in the moments, provide a glimpse of hope and healing to one of life's most difficult experiences: marital betrayal. She shares honest and raw memories of times that drew her into a closer relationship with God, and called upon her to search deep within to find stability during the initial period of shock and disbelief. Practical suggestions for moving through the grief provide encouragement from becoming stuck and immobilized. Stephanie sprinkles in humor and moments of joy she found within the weeks after confession, giving you permission to continue to live and experience happiness that balances the hard work of healing.

This hope-filled guide will meet those in the immediate aftermath of confession, as well as the woman who is months or years along in the journey and yet still searching to find further healing and freedom from the pain.

- **Christie Hunter,** *MA, R.C.C.; Co-Founder Theravive.com*

Through Grief and Pain to Whole-Hearted Healing

With authenticity and an unflinching look back on her own marriage crisis, Stephanie Broersma has crafted a Bible study guide for women who suffer betrayal by a spouse. When her own marriage was threatened by her husband's infidelity and struggles with pornography, Stephanie was shattered to discover very little guidance in Christian circles. She learned that many women in her situation suffer in silence, and that the Church is not always a supportive or safe place for women whose husbands are unfaithful.

2 Corinthians 1:4 says that God comforts us in all our troubles, so that we can comfort others with the same Godly comfort. Based on her own journey with God through grief and pain, to whole-hearted healing and restoration of her marriage, Stephanie created a ministry to help other women. This Bible study is the result of her search of Scripture to find comfort and direction, and incorporates the questions and experiences of many women who face this painful situation.

With respect for God's word and compassion for all parties involved, Stephanie guides women as they process through the natural emotions of shock, grief, self-blame, and anger, and gives them hope and positive direction for the future. Stephanie's own marriage survived, and thrived, after rising from the ashes of infidelity and shame. This study will be a comfort and encouragement to others on the journey.

- **Ramona Stumpf,** *Director of Life-Changers, North County Christ the King Community Church*

A Journey From Personal Devastation to Restoration

Stephanie Broersma has been Reclaimed! This Study Guide is a window to her soul, giving a full view of the pain, brokenness and heartache caused by betrayal in her marriage. Stephanie is vulnerable, honest and inviting in the way that she shares her journey from personal devastation to restoration. I have been honored to witness Stephanie allow God to create beauty from ashes through the power of forgiveness and grace.

Embrace her words of empathy and understanding as she identifies feelings yet unnamed in your heart. This is a must-read for anyone needing to be Reclaimed from the pain of betrayal.

- **Kurt Langstraat,** MA; Senior Pastor, *North County Christ the King Community Church*; Lynden, Washington

From *Reclaimed Small Group* Attendees:

Reclaimed is a safe space to begin the journey of wholeness after the unthinkable has happened. Knowing that I'm not alone in the pain I've experienced has been a true comfort. The Bible-based material we studied helped me start the pathway to healing and forgiveness, and reminded me that I can trust and rely on God, who will never let me down.

- **Small Group Attendee**

Through this group, I've been challenged to seek Him (Jesus) first and take the focus off the hurt around me so He can call me out on everything that takes the focus off of Him. While any change can seem difficult, the reward for doing the hard work is immeasurable when it comes to deeply being challenged daily to refuse anything less than being seen as 'the daughter of the King Most High.

- **Small group Attendee**

Related Materials

- Reclaimed Small Group Leaders Guide
- Reclaimed: Finding Your Identity after Marital Betrayal
- Reclaimed Blessings Journal

> Thank you for your purchase of the Reclaimed Study Guide! All supplemental materials for the Reclaimed Small Group are written into the course and available upon request. Contact **stephanie@reclaimedministry.com** to request your digital file and we'll get them to you free of charge.
>
> Reclaimed Ministry would love to help get you into the network of those leading groups around the country and women processing with others in small groups, praying for great healing and wholeness.
>
> To skip straight to the small group materials, scroll to page 17. Prior to that is my story, which gives you context into how and why Reclaimed Ministry was developed. I'm honored to help guide you through the small group process as well, so make sure to reach out with any questions or if you're interested in Reclaimed Leadership Training.
>
> Blessings,
> Stephanie Broersma

Reclaimed Small Group Guide

A Course To Guide You Through Betrayal Within Your Marriage

By **Stephanie Broersma**

ISBN: 978-179-138-2865

Cover Design by Lisa DenBleyker, Lynden, WA and Chad Williams, Lynden, WA. Printed in the United States. For more information, contact:

Reclaimed Ministry
Stephanie Broersma
P.O. Box 569
Lynden, Washington, 98264
United States of America

To learn more about Reclaimed Ministry and related materials, visit:
www.reclaimedministry.com
@reclaimedministry

Table of Contents:

Dedication

To my sweet older sister, Traci, my biggest cheerleader.
I can hear you still, cheering me on from heaven.
To the women who have, and continue to trust me with their stories.
And to my husband Tim, who continues to pursue me daily.

Introduction
A Normal Girl with an Unexpected Story

"Come and listen, all you who fear God; let me tell you
what He has done for me."

Psalm 66:16; NIV

My childhood was quite textbook, according to what North American society standards were and how ordinary families were perceived on TV in the 1980s. I grew up in a Christian home with two parents, Paul and Cheryl, who were and still are, forty years later, dedicated to family, work, and providing stability within our home unit. The greatest gift my parents gave me was the blessing of a two-parent home. Yes, I heard and saw fights like any normal married couple has in their years together, but our home was always secure, safe, and loving.

Girl Meets Boy

Tim Broersma and I had no intention of dating in high school. That didn't stop me from admiring him. As a freshman, I thought he was so cute, I even wrote him a love letter. Oh, to be young and naïve! I'm not sure what my intentions were in writing that silly letter, but his sister Becky was my best friend and, being new to the school, generally trusted what she had to say. She talked a lot about her brother, and when Tim finally tried to ask me out, didn't give him the chance to complete his sentence. "No," I blurted. "Becky said to say no!" I'm so grateful for that advice.

We made our separate ways through high school. I had just graduated when our paths crossed again. This time something sparked between us, and we began a "just friends" phase that lasted about three to four months. worked at Goldie's Bar and Grill that summer, and to my surprise, I would often find notes, gifts, or Tim by my car waiting for me to finish my shift. We spent many hours at the local diner Shari's, sitting over a cup of coffee or hot chocolate, discussing life, breakups, and, most often, the topic of faith.

We spent countless hours chatting the summer evenings away just as friends. It wasn't until I moved down to Seattle for college that things started to change, and the thought of being apart became unbearable.

Marriage to Honeymoon in Paris

Tim and I dated for a few years before he asked me to marry him. From the proposal to the wedding ceremony, everything was perfect. We honeymooned in Paris, then traveled to Scandinavia over our first-year anniversary with the semi-professional barbershop quartet Tim was a part of.

Time passed, and we were secure in our jobs, living comfortably in our first home. It was a fixer-upper, but it was ours. Tim's five-year plan—to hold off on children for five years—lasted all but two years, when our firstborn daughter Addison arrived. After some hard discussions, Tim and I sold our first home and moved into a rental home for two years. Tim and I worked really well together. We shared many of the responsibilities within our business and our home without fighting or arguing.

I noticed nothing out of the normal until my second pregnancy. That was in 2008, the same time we were moving to our current home. I was three months pregnant and having complications with the pregnancy.

I began to notice a distance between us—our touch and communications were off. I can count on one hand how many times we were sexually intimate during the pregnancy.

Through the duration of my pregnancy, Tim became increasingly busy with his work. My belly was growing, and the end date was near. Our little Charlie was born three weeks early via c-section. In the moments before my surgery, Tim was busy typing on his computer, while the nurse poked me five times to start the IV. I remember looking over at him, tears welling, searching for comfort.

Charlie was born with lung and breathing problems, and they kept him in the nursery for a full twenty-four hours. Because my blood pressure was extremely low, the nurses wouldn't allow me out of bed. Consequently, I was shown only pictures of my little man cub. Depression crept closer to me. When I was finally cleared to go to Charlie, other family members had already touched, smelled, and kissed his little cheeks—but I was given only five minutes to quickly visit, and then was sent back to bed. When the nurses finally brought Charlie to my room, Tim lay sleeping on the couch. He was so into his work, he even had contractors meeting him outside my hospital room. The first time Addi saw her brother, my Mom was there, not Tim.

I didn't recognize my postpartum depression until after it had passed. Neither did I notice how far away my husband was until it was too late.

By the time Charlie was six months old, the cloud of depression had lifted. At the same time, Tim was sharing an office with his business partner, Greg, and they had conversations about the book of Revelation. Tim's secret was still unknown, but something Greg said slam-dunked my husband into a breaking moment. After that conversation, Tim began feverishly searching for a scripture that would allow him to confess his sins to Jesus but not have to be completely honest with me, his wife. This search went on for six months, but in the process gave way to a new man. Tim recommitted his life to Christ, and things on the outside were changing.

I saw more engagement at home when we lay in bed and prayed. I didn't have to prod him to pray—he offered it willingly. We were reading devotions and experiencing true worship together. Our communication consistently improved—we still never yelled or fought with each other; we simply worked out issues or differences. I felt loved. I felt cherished. I trusted our relationship and the patterns we had made over seven years of marriage.

Deleted Conversations

One day, I opened a Facebook message and found deleted threads of conversation not appropriate within a marriage. I felt instant panic. Fear paralyzed me as I recognized what I was reading. It can't be, I thought. My gut told me there was more and I knew.

Tim later confessed to a ten-year pornography addiction that started back in high school. And then he confessed to extramarital affairs—yes, plural!—that took place during my second pregnancy. My spirit was crushed.

All I had was my faith in Christ—and as I looked to Him to guide me, I had no idea what the next steps toward healing would be, nor did I know how to respond the next time I saw my husband. Even as my world crumbled, I was determined to fight for us, for our marriage and I refused to allow Satan to turn our marriage into another dismal statistic.

We kept our marriage collapse extremely private until two years after Tim's confession. At that time, our church asked if we would be willing to share our testimonies via video. We did, and the response that followed was incredible. We received notes of encouragement for stepping out and sharing our story. Tim and I were asked to speak at local churches, on radio talk shows, at marriage retreats, and to share our story on national television.

The very thing that made me crawl into a fetal position and cry until I had no more tears, the thing that had offered no hope of repair—God used to bring hope to others in similar situations. I began meeting regularly with women at local coffee shops and through text messages and emails. Long phone calls spent listening, praying with women, and connecting them to the right resources in their area became frequent. And I discovered a common thread running through my communications with hurting women—they felt they had no one to go to in their own church; there was no group or resource that provided real, tangible advice and support for broken women.

People started asking why I hadn't started yet. When I was going to get a group going? I resisted at first, until a mentor challenged me by lighting a fire under my seat. "Why not?" She urged. "Write your own curriculum; get it going."

An Ugly Topic

The more I heard about the lack of support for women like me in their local churches, the more frustrated I grew. Some women were told, "Be quiet; it's your fault your husband went elsewhere." Others were told, "Don't say anything to anyone. It's not pornography unless it's in front of a computer." This was appalling! The need to educate and encourage women on their journey toward healing became so evident to me that I had no choice but to act.

God made it very clear to me during the months of healing and reconstruction that followed Tim's betrayal, what my future purpose would be in life. It is now my heart's passion to speak out about my darkest days and to share the hope God offered in my brokenness, during the worst time of my life.

My prayer is that you will see in this 30 Day Personal Journal the same divine web that held me up when my two feet were too weak to stand and that you will find the same hope I experienced through the cross of Christ. Nothing is too messy or too far gone that God cannot restore. With Him by your side, you can deal with the pain inside and the muck outside. And you can walk with your head held high, offering God all the glory for the amazing, reclaimed story of your life.

A Daughter of the King

I am not a professional in the area of marriage and betrayal. I can't offer you "30 Easy Steps to Overcoming the Betrayal Game." I'm simply a girl with a story who dedicates herself to parenting, keeping the washing machine running, placing edible somethings on our dinner plates . . . and keeping the passion alive in our marriage. I don't have a bunch of letters that follow my name, nor do I have a degree hanging on my wall that qualifies me for this task. I don't claim to have it all together, and certainly, there are days when our home would benefit from more structure. I'm weak when it comes to sweets, still struggle with how I view myself, and will be the first to tell you if things are not okay. What I do know is this; I am a daughter of the King who loves me regardless of my weaknesses or strengths. God saw that I was capable of the task to help others, and He has given me a voice to extend hope to lives of women who are shattered from marital infidelity.

My husband cherishes me as his bride and loves me more every day. I trust in us, in who we have become together, and will stand up for our marriage any day of the week. My faith got me here today, and my faith will carry me through tomorrow. My hope for you—as a reader, leader, or broken woman—is that you will find how deeply you are loved by your Savior and that you are not alone in this moment.

How did God heal me? That's what I am going to share with you and here are some practical ways to use this book:

1. **This is your story.** I challenge you to keep the focus on your heart as you answer the Personal Reflection section in your small group and invite God into your journey with the understanding you can't change those within your sphere.
2. **Don't rush the process and become overwhelmed.** If it's too much, try answering one reflection question and choose one scripture to meditate on from the scripture section throughout the week.
3. **Put your armor on.** You are entering a spiritual battle that the enemy wants nothing more than for you to fail miserably at as you desire to reclaim truth in your life. Read the armor passage in Ephesians 6:10-18 out loud in prayer every day.
4. **Be in prayer.** Prayer is vital even on a good day. Asking a friend or mentor to cover you in prayer as you process what you are reading.
5. **Seek God's blessings.** Grab a Reclaimed Blessing Journal (info in the Resource Section) and write down the ways God is reminding you of his goodness and faithfulness. Journal your prayer requests and highlight the ways God responds to your requests. Focus on the beauty of your journey through your words. Share with those in your group!
6. **Get connected.** You may feel like you're doing this alone but that's not God's plan for life to be lived alone. Join the Reclaimed Ministry Community in a closed group on Facebook. You can find out more at www.reclaimedministry.com

Stephanie Broersma
June 2018
Lynden, Washington

"To bestow on them a crown of beauty instead of ashes, the oil of gladness instead of mourning, and a garment of praise instead of a spirit of despair. They will be called oaks of righteousness. Instead of their shame my people will receive a double portion, and instead of disgrace they will rejoice in their inheritance; and so they will inherit a double portion in their land, and everlasting joy will be theirs."

Isaiah 61:3,7

Purpose

The purpose of Reclaimed is to help women find hope and healing amidst the pain and suffering caused by betrayal in their marriages. Our hope is that God would set a fire in our hearts to become more passionate, find greater joy, and an intimacy never thought deserved. As we dive into the Word and hold each other **accountable**, may we in **confidence** seek truth, speak out of **respect**, **protect** each others stories and always **give God the glory** for even the smallest of baby steps towards complete restoration in our hearts. I pray that you will find beauty in the pile of ashes before you and be redeemed through grace, and receive the double portion set before you.

{ Reminders }

- speak out of respect for our marriages, spouses, and ourselves
- keep each others comments, questions, and stories confidential
- share with an open heart but with God's intentions in consideration
- respect each others emotions
- walk in humility, forgiveness, and with love

Our Commitment

In order to get the most out of this study, we commit to allow God to open old wounds, showing us where growth is needed, forgiveness can be spoken, and attempts at healing accepted. God is ready to do big things in our hearts and marriages if we're willing to let Him.

When you reflect back to the raw moments in the betrayal of your vow, what are some of the emotions, the feelings you experienced? {betrayal, mistrust, rejection, embarrassment, shame, violation, unworthy, dirty, defeated, humiliation, angry, outraged, frustrated, dismay, crushed, deceived, dishonesty, shock}. Over the next twelve weeks, we will walk through the hurt caused by betrayal. Our focus will be on **CHOOSING** to see God in the pain, and learning to trust in God's promise for His cherished, beloved daughters as we build a body of support, encouragement, and prayer around each other.

Course Outline:

The Initial Shock & Betrayal
Betrayal, Bitterness, Shame

Navigating Grief & Exhaustion
Grief, Weariness, Image

The Choice to Forgive
Forgiveness, Hope, Trust

Educating Our Realities
Education, Communication, Support

A Restored Smile
Restoration, Redeemed, Joy

Perspective Moving Forward
Boundaries, Perspective, Dating

If you have any questions, comments, needs or would like to chat a bit longer about a topic, please contact:

Reclaimed Ministry

P.O. Box 569

Lynden, WA 98264

stephanie@reclaimedministry.com

www.reclaimedministry.com

@reclaimedministry

Betrayal

A whisper from God...

"My dear sweet child, I know your pain. right now I want you to know I am here with you in that pain. As you struggle to breathe, remember I am the breath of your life. I breathe new life into you. I control the wind and the water. I am in control of your situation. I have not left you alone - I am here with you.

Take my comfort and wrap it around you like a blanket giving you warmth. Turn to me even though you may feel I am far away. I am here with you. Let me take your pain and heal you. Let me take your pain and make you stronger. Draw near to me and I will give you My strength. Let me be all you need right now. Give it all to me and I will take your pain and give you my peace.

Because I love you more than anything - I AM HERE FOR YOU..." [1]

The book *The Myth of the Greener Grass* by J. Allan Petersen, has a great illustration of what some of us may be feeling right now. It goes like this...

"A little boy was asked by his father to say grace at the table. While the rest of the family watched, the little guy eyed every dish of food his mother had prepared. After the examination he bowed his head and honestly prayed, "Lord, I don't like the looks of it, but I thank you for it and I'll eat it anyway. Amen." [2]

"A little lie is like a little pregnancy - it doesn't take long before everyone knows."
- C.S. Lewis

"Every lie creates distance between relationships."
- David Powlison

When you are at your _____ point, your only other option is to _____ on God.

No betrayal looks the same and can sneak up on a person through gossip, lies, actions or the lack of engagement. Since Adam and Eve betrayed God, and allowed sin to enter our world, betrayal has been almost unavoidable as one of the primary delivery mechanisms for sin. You may be thinking, "I'll never get over it. What happened to me was so wrong. It hurt so much. I've been scarred so deeply by betrayal and brutality. My anger rages like a nuclear furnace inside me. It seems as permanent, as destructive, and as deep as the hurt."

The Bible is full of examples of betrayal:

- Jesus was betrayed. Judas betrayed Jesus after years of sharing meals, talking, praying and laughing together. **Psalm 41:9** *"Even my close friend, whom I trusted, he who shared my bread, has lifted up his heel against me."*

- We read in **Isaiah 53:3**, *"He was despised and rejected by men, a man of sorrows, and familiar with suffering."*

- **John 13:2**, *"Jesus was troubled in spirit and testified, "I tell you the truth, one of you is going to betray me."*

- Absalom betrayed his father David. *(2 Samuel 15-19)*

Those closest to Jesus were the ones that hurt Him the most. Sometimes physical pain is less painful than the words spoken against you. I would imagine that when the rooster cried three times over, the betrayal Jesus experienced is much like the pain a wife experiences in the midst of betrayal within her vow. Jesus knows our pains. He became man and understands our hurts, anxieties, and our deepest flesh wounds. There is nothing Jesus doesn't understand, and He is waiting to be your Friend in the darkness.

Betrayal is ugly. If you ignore it, like a weed it will corrupt your foundation and cause bitterness to tear your life apart. Don't allow the pain to determine your tomorrow. God's Word is truth and it will fertilize your soul, remove your bitterness, and bring light to the darkness.

Part of healing is being able to see _____ the betrayal and allow it to bond you _____ to your spouse. This is not a fast food fix; there is no easy fix to heal the pain from betrayal. God challenges us to crucify the flesh and turn the other cheek.

Betrayal becomes the _____ to our situation. (see Three Trees Diagram) The situation does not **make** us who we are. The situation **reveals** who we are.

Tim Jackson writes for the ministry now is recognized as Our Daily Bread. Here is a little of what his article "When A Spouse Is Unfaithful" has to say which can be found in the back of your binder.

"No words adequately describe the trauma a person suffers when a spouse's affair is exposed. Many report that it is the most dreadful thing they have ever faced - more excruciating than losing a parent, being diagnosed with cancer, or being fired.

An affair infects a vicious wound to the heart of a faithful spouse. Wounded spouses often feel, "While I may look the same on the outside, inside I'm hemorrhaging and I can't stop it." Most betrayed spouses feel as if they are going crazy - especially during the initial stages of shock.

Gone is the sense of being intact and whole. Self-respect is shattered and those betrayed commonly ask themselves, " Why didn't I speak up earlier when I sensed something was wrong?"

Betrayal can strip the heart of any sense of constancy, security, and meaning. Feelings of being used, discarded, and rejected replace feelings of being chosen, special, and valued." [3]

Questions for Discussion and Reflection:

- Are you able to locate the heat in your life? How do you see God when the pressure is on and the heat of the situation is overwhelming? What do you run to?

- In your moment of shock, did you hear God's still small voice? If not, do you think He wasn't there? Do you feel betrayal from God?

- When you are faced with a trigger, how do you respond and communicate your worries with your spouse? If the marriage ended in divorce, how have you been able to deal with triggers? What are your buttons?

- Betrayal looks different to everyone. How did/does it look like to you? Are you a vengeance-taker or are you transformed to do courageous good in the face of evil?

- How did God face betrayal and overcome the doubts of believers and followers?

What Does the Bible Say?

- **Proverbs 25:9,** "If you argue your case with a neighbor, do not betray another man's confidence."

- **2 Chronicles 26:16,** "But after Uzziah became powerful, his pride led to his downfall. He was unfaithful to the Lord his God."

- **Luke 22:54-62,** "Then seizing him, they led him away and took him into the house of the high priest. Peter followed at a distance. And when some there had kindled a fire in the middle of the courtyard and had sat down together, Peter sat down with them. A servant girl saw him seated there in the firelight. She looked closely at him and said, "This man was with him." But he denied it. "Woman, I don't know him," he said. A little later someone else saw him and said, "You also are one of them." "Man, I am not!" Peter replied. About an hour later another asserted, "Certainly this fellow was with him, for he is a Galilean." Peter replied, "Man, I don't know what you're talking about!" Just as he was speaking, the rooster crowed. The Lord turned and looked straight at Peter. Then Peter remembered the word the Lord had spoken to him: "Before the rooster crows today, you will disown me three times." And he went outside and wept bitterly."

- **Psalm 41:9**, "Even my close friend, someone I trusted, one who shared my bread, has turned against me."

- **Deuteronomy 32:15**, "Jeshurun grew fat and kicked; filled with food, they became heavy and sleek. They abandoned the God who made them and rejected the Rock their Savior."

- **Proverbs 27:6**, "Wounds from a friend can be trusted, but an enemy multiplies kisses."

- **Matthew 5:9-11**, "Blessed are the peacemakers, for they will be called children of God. Blessed are those who are persecuted because of righteousness, for theirs is the kingdom of heaven. Blessed are you when people insult you, persecute you and falsely say all kinds of evil against you because of me."

- **Matthew 5:38-48**, "You have heard that it was said, 'Eye for eye, and tooth for tooth.' But I tell you, do not resist an evil person. If anyone slaps you on the right cheek, turn to them the other cheek also. And if anyone wants to sue you and take your shirt, hand over your coat as well. If anyone forces you to go one mile, go with them two miles. Give to the one who asks you, and do not turn away from the one who wants to borrow from you. You have heard that it was said, 'Love your neighbor and hate your enemy.' But I tell you, love your enemies and pray for those who persecute you, that you may be children of your Father in heaven. He causes his sun to rise on the evil and the good, and sends rain on the righteous and the unrighteous. If you love those who love you, what reward will you get? Are not even the tax collectors doing that? And if you greet only your own people, what are you doing more than others? Do not even pagans do that? Be perfect, therefore, as your heavenly Father is perfect."

- **Lamentations 1:3,19**, "After affliction and harsh labor, Judah has gone into exile. She dwells among the nations; she finds no resting place. All who pursue her have overtaken her in the midst of her distress. I called to my allies but they betrayed me. My priests and my elders perished in the city while they searched for food to keep themselves alive."

    * These verses are talking about the betrayal of the nation and the people who should have been of help were they themselves in trouble. Nelson's Compact Bible Commentary says: "The book of Lamentations reveals the broken heart of the prophet Jeremiah over the national tragedy that had

unfolded before his eyes; Jerusalem, God's city, had fallen to the Babylonians. The people of Israel had chosen to reject God. Yet even in this time of suffering there was hope. The Lord would not discipline His people forever; He would eventually restore those who waited on Him.

The scriptures tackle some of the toughest questions faced by God's people: How can God's love and justice be reconciled with our pain? If God is in control of history, how can a nation suffer so much? Where was God during His people's unhappiest hour? The anger of God is a sign that He cares. The Lord's anger is never unreasonable. Even in His display of anger, God is still full of mercy and grace. His faithfulness is the greatest comfort to those who suffer." [4]

و

Betrayal and Bitterness can cause us to hear things differently as we mix the facts with the negative opinions of those facts. With Hollywood making affairs seem like a romantic escape filled with opportunities and success, we can easily allow our minds to create a fantasy of what happened. Society has quickly accepted this attitude and places instant blame on the spouse left in shambles. Be aware of the facts so you don't fall into Satan's trap to deceive your mind and cause you to believe lies.

We are told...Fact:	We hear...Negative Opinion:
"My husband loves another woman."	"I'm ugly and not worthy of his love."
"I was deceived in my marriage."	"I will never be able to trust him again."
"The betrayal hurts so deeply."	"I will never forgive or be healed."
"This has never happened in my family before."	"Our reputation is destroyed."
"Our marriage has failed."	"I'm a terrible wife and mother."

Your entire thought process will become distorted and inaccurate when under stress and turmoil. Make sure you separate the facts from fantasy.

Brokenness, or despair, can be detected in tears and death, in suffering and agony, damage and decay which could result in anger or greed, selfishness or loneliness or even despair.

Bitterness

*"Forgiveness is agreeing to live with the consequences of another person's sin. You are going to live with those consequences anyway whether you like it or not, so the only choice you have is whether you will do so in the **bondage of bitterness** or in the **freedom of forgiveness**. It may seem unfair and you may wonder where the justice is in it, but justice is found at the cross, which makes forgiveness legally and morally right.*

Jesus took the eternal consequences of sin upon Himself. God "made Him who knew no sin to be sin on our behalf, that we might become the righteousness of God in Him". (2 Corinthians 5:21) We, however, often suffer the temporary consequences of other people's sins. That is simply a harsh reality of life all of us have to face."

Neil T. Anderson
The Bondage Breaker [5]

Christ left no room for bitterness when He died on the cross to save us from our sins. Big or small. It's all the same to God, but as humans we give our sins a scale rating and make the smaller ones seem like a lesser evil compared to the ultimate betrayal of our marriage vows. Bitterness will seep into every area of your life, if not forgiven. I've witnessed people divorced for over 30 years still holding grudges against each other due to hearts not allowing forgiveness, friendships ended because of bitter roots, and marriages on the edge of collapse because it's just "too hard" to face the pain and trudge through the emotions. **Bitterness is satan's deceit that robs us of joy.**

Another way the devil uses bitterness is by empowering those who have been hurt to become historic with their spouse. By that I mean in the middle of an argument you yell out in frustration and hurt, "I feel this way because YOU did this to me. It's your fault I'm having a bad day. I did this because you did it first!" Bitterness will show up if forgiveness is not spoken. Like that nasty weed that will keep coming back if not cut at the root, bitterness will continue to resurface if not handled.

We need to remember that we are _____ capable of sinful actions and we all need grace given to us as well. "For _____ have sinned and fall short of the glory of God." Romans 3:23

Betrayal is the _____; bitterness becomes one of the revolving _____ that produces bad fruit and pulls us away from Christ.

Questions for Discussion and Reflection:

- In what ways have revolving consequences pulled you away from God?

- What bitterness do you have in your life that needs to be brought to the foot of the cross?

- What joy has satan robbed you of?

- How has releasing your bitterness to the cross set you free and how did God redeem you through that process of forgiveness?

Testimony from a woman who attended our small group:

"I wanted to tell you that at our last meeting, I think God gave me this picture in my mind of a garden. A beautiful garden representing my marriage. And a weed popped up in the garden, which is bitterness. Like you said, in the beginning of betrayal, bitterness will almost be automatic, but it's what we do with it. Sometimes I choose to sit in front of this weed and tell myself the whole garden is ruined. I don't enjoy the rest of the flowers, or the fruits growing. This weed was put there by the enemy, but it won't grow unless we water it and tend to it (i.e. nurse it). If I do pay too much attention to it, water it, nurse it, it will grow quickly. It will take over my entire garden. And if I sit in front of this weed all the time and ignore the rest of the garden, the beautiful flowers will eventually die too. The weed also needs sun to survive, so the way I kill it off is to put it in the shadow of the cross. In the darkness, without water, it won't survive…and my garden will flourish once again. There may be other weeds that pop up every now and again, but I will still be able to enjoy my garden. I'm learning how to reject the lies the enemy tells, and to choose not to focus on the bitterness, but instead on the good works God is doing in my marriage."

What Does the Bible Say?

- **Psalm 71:20,** "Though You have made me see troubles, many and bitter, You will restore my life again; from the depths of the earth You will bring me up."

- **Ephesians 4:31,** "Get rid of all bitterness, rage and anger, brawling and slander, along with every form of malice."

- **James 3:14-15,** "But if you harbor bitter envy and selfish ambition in your hearts, do not boast about it or deny the truth. Such "wisdom" does not come down from Heaven but is earthly, unspiritual, of the devil."

- **Hebrews 12:15,** "See to it that no one misses the grace of God and that no bitter root grows up to cause trouble and defile many."

- **Romans 12:17-21,** "Do not repay anyone evil for evil. Be careful to do what is right in the eyes of everybody. If it is possible, as far as it depends on you, live at peace with everyone. Do not take revenge, my friends, but leave room for God's wrath, for it is written: "It is mine to avenge; I will repay," says the Lord. On the contrary: "If your enemy is hungry, feed him; if he is thirsty, give him something to drink. In doing this, you will heap burning coals soon his head."

- **Proverbs 14:10,** " Each heart knows its own bitterness, and no one can share its joy."

Shame

We have to consciously make a _____ to not let the shame creep over our wounds and make scars of _____ or it will separate us from Jesus, isolating us from His plan. At times, it may feel like there is a sign on your back that says: "My spouse betrayed our wedding vows", as shame is like an article of clothing that covers you with embarrassment, guilt, and seems to overwhelm your emotions.

Shame is satan's way of silencing you. It tells us we're not good enough for Jesus or others. Shame caused by betrayal can be paralyzing; it can strip you of every positive thought, memory and celebration you shared with your spouse. Secrecy, silence and self-judgement creates intense disappointment and makes us feel unworthy. There were days where I (Stephanie) caught myself glancing at photographs of our family from pre-confession questioning whether a peek at a pornographic image happened on that trip or in this place of our home. I'd think to myself, "I wonder if something happened when we were here or there? When he came home from this business trip, were the gifts given because of guilt for actions that took place earlier?" As I reviewed our memories, feelings of shame for not protecting my husband at certain vacation spots would overwhelm me. Or opposite, I'd become curious and question the timeline of the addiction and piece together conversations at that moment.

A 2014 article posted on the website, WIRED, written by Christian Jarrett, said this about brain research which is trying to prove that shame / humiliation is the most intense human emotion:

> "Otten and Jonas (a pair of psychologists) said, that shame & humiliation, more than the other emotions they studied, leads to a mobilization of more processing power and a greater consumption of mental resources. This supports the idea that humiliation is a particularly intense and demanding negative emotional experience that has far-reaching consequences for individuals and groups alike. The brain seems to be doing more when you're feeling humiliated, but we don't really know what. One possibility, which in fairness they acknowledge, is that humiliation requires more mental processing, not because it's so intense, but because it's a complex social emotion that involves monitoring loss of social status." [6]

It's no wonder we're so wiped when trying to navigate the emotions and burdens of betrayal, and working through the shame and humiliation it has caused us. We need to be aware that Satan is using this shame and humiliation to render us useless in the moment, and to pull us away from the only thing that can provide the healing we require - Jesus.

There should be no shame in coming before our Savior in these moments, even as raw and ugly as we may feel. God does not judge us for simply feeling. God walks by our side as we work through the emotions of the pain caused against us. Don't let Satan take that experience from you.

<u>**Questions for Discussion and Reflection:**</u>

- How has shame robbed your heart? How have you been silenced? Who do you blame for the shame in your life? Remember, God created our nervous system, which includes our emotions, so He knows what we're feeling and experiencing in our shame and pain.

- In what ways have you been able to bring your guilt for your shame to the cross? Being able to recognize cross roads (guilt & shame) and building Godly character out of it is a huge accomplishment. Jesus wants to show up in our shame.

- Has shame changed your lifestyle and your perspective of yourself?

- How do you communicate shame? Silent treatment, cold shoulder, retaliation through negative actions isolation?

What Does the Bible Say?

- **Isaiah 50:7**, "Because the Sovereign Lord helps me, I will not be disgraced. Therefore I have set my face like flint, and I know I will not be put to shame."

- **Isaiah 61:7**, "Instead of their shame my people will receive a double portion, and instead of disgrace they will rejoice in their inheritance; and so they will inherit a double portion in their land, and everlasting joy will be theirs."

- **1 John 1:9**, "If we confess our sins, he is faithful and just and will forgive us our sins and purify us from all unrighteousness."

- **Genesis 3:10**, "He (Adam) answered, "I heard you in the garden, and I was afraid because I was naked so I hid."

- **Psalm 34:4-5,** "I sought the Lord, and he answered me; he delivered me from all my fears. Those who look to him are radiant; their faces are never covered in shame."

- **Romans 10:11**, "As the Scriptures says, Anyone who trusts in him will never be put to shame."

- **Isaiah 29:22**, "Therefore this is what the Lord, who redeemed Abraham, says to the house of Jacob: "No longer will Jacob be ashamed; no longer will their faces grow pale."

Grief

"Jesus wept." (John 11:35) In that action alone, God gave us _____ to grieve over what **WE** love. This is an important step to take in our journey to healing. **Tears are okay**; it's healthy to let it out rather than bottle everything up inside. Grieve over what was lost and stolen from your relationship. Grieve over the sacred being ripped out of your marriage. Use the emotions to positively propel you forward instead of what some so often do, and stay stuck in the muck. God does allow us to grieve, but, He wants us to find JOY!

That first night, I was told, "Grieve over the death of your marriage. Grieve over the loss of what was, what could have been, and what may be. Your marriage will never look the same and for that you need to grieve for what you lost." Don't think for a minute that you don't have permission or you're on a timeline of grieving. This process looks different for each person and is a vital step to healing and restoration.

Seven Stages of Grief:

1.
2.
3.
4.
5.
6.
7.

Did you know that "DO NOT FEAR" is the most common command in the Bible?[7] As you grieve, consider your destination. Jesus teaches that we will be delivered from evil in all its forms. Don't skip this critical process and stage in your healing journey, but also, don't loose sight of the end matter. (Ecclesiastes 7:8)

Questions for Discussion and Reflection:

- Did you find it hard to grieve, with bitterness lurking around the corner, or did God give you the grace to journey through this step with compassion?

- What negative fruits have birthed out of the grief and betrayal in your marriage? Are you able to recognize the bad fruits, and if so, what are you doing to change them?

- How can we grieve for others without showing guilt (we can show guilt through body language and conversations) for their sins?

What Does the Bible Say?

- **Isaiah 49:13,** "Shout for joy, O heavens; rejoice, O earth; burst into song, O mountains! For the Lord comforts His people and will have compassion on His afflicted ones."

- **Isaiah 43:2,** "When you pass through waters, I will be with you; and when you pass through the rivers, they will not sweep over you. When you walk through the fire, you will not be burned; the flames will not set you ablaze."

- **Matthew 5:4**, "Blessed are those who mourn, for they will be comforted."

- **1 Peter 5:7**, "Cast all your anxiety on Him because He cares for you."

- **Revelation 21:4,** "He will wipe every tear from their eyes. There will be no more death or mourning or crying or pain, for the old order of things has passed away."

Weariness

The moment you stop trying to fix things yourself and _____ your need for Him is the moment He shows up to give you _____.

Exhaustion can make us do very funny things, or even stupid things too! I once put a gallon of milk in the cereal cupboard and cereal in the fridge. I was deprived of sleep from spending nearly 4 weeks on the couch with two kids; I was pouring into them so that the situation didn't overwhelm them. I was slowly starting to eat and drink again, attempting a light work schedule and spending many late nights in deep, lengthy renewing conversations with my husband and Jesus. Exhaustion overcame me and depression was lurking around the corner.

In our fast-paced life of jobs, family, relationships, and the household chore list, we find ourselves exhausted at the end of a day, before we even add on the emotional despair that accompanies a broken marriage. It is easy to think that a quick prayer before falling asleep will remedy this exhaustion, but God wants more of us in those weak moments. God will give us the energy to push forward when we allow Him to fuel up our hearts and minds. Making it a habit to start the day and end the day with God, as well as walking with him throughout the day, is just as vital to survival as water. Frankly, it's more vital! Even if you have no strength to get out of bed, find the words to utter a simple plea to the One who is ready to fill you with living sustaining words.

God's _____ really is enough to carry _____ when you feel like _____ can't walk anymore.

Questions for Discussion and Reflection:

- Do you carve out time each day to spend with God?

- What are some of the "good fruit" that you have been able to notice from your situation? Do you find it hard to produce good fruit when you feel depleted and worn out?

- Are you able to recognize your fatigue, and humble yourself enough to ask for help?

- What are your essentials to a weary day? Do you rely on your faith to get you through or does your faith need some "working out" so the exhaustion doesn't take over?

What Does the Bible Say?

- **Matthew 11:28,** "Come to Me, all who are weary burdened, and I will give you rest."

- **Psalm 62:1-2,** "My soul finds rest in God alone; my salvation does from Him. He alone is my rock and salvation; He is my fortress, I will never be shaken."

- **Romans 12:11,** "Never be lacking in zeal, but keep your spiritual fervor, serving the Lord."

- **Hebrews 12:3,** "Consider Him who endured such opposition from sinful men, so that you will not grow weary and lose heart."

- **Galatians 6:9,** "Let us not become weary in doing good, for at the proper time we will reap a harvest if we do not give up."

- **Isaiah 40:31**, "But those who hope in the Lord will renew their strength. They will soar on wings like eagles; they will run and not grow weary, they will walk and not be faint."

- **Nehemiah 9:20**, "You gave your good Spirit to instruct them. You did not withhold your manna from their mouths, and you gave them water for their thirst."

Image

*When we don't realize who we are in Christ, **our faith will be crippled.** If you don't feel worthy to exercise your authority in Christ, then you won't be doing it in the fullness of faith and will lack assurance. Satan works diligently to program people's minds to feel unworthy and unable to walk in power of God here on earth. This is one of the most popular strongholds in existence today in the body of Christ! The truth is that we, by our own power and effort, are unworthy, but it is the Blood of Christ that makes us worthy. And if we say we are unworthy when the Blood says we are, then we are denying the work that Christ did for us on the cross!*

- Online article [8]

It is critical to know _____ _____ _____ in Christ as you offer yourself to your marriage. Husband and wife need to have _____ relationships with their risen Savior and _____ _____, share a Christ-like union in their vows. If not, you will find yourself lost, drained, and depleted of everything you are. Being able to stand strong in your presentation and depiction of God is an important aspect of the shared relationship. Your _____ is NOT found in the sins of the past or web of _____ from the mistakes in your marriage. Your identity is _____ in the risen _____!

The majority of women walking through betrayal have expressed how devastated their self-image is after picking up the shattered pieces of their marriage. This has been the most challenging sin consequence resulting from Tim's confession. Here's how mislead my ideas of image were right after Tim's confession....

The first Sunday we went to church together after Tim had moved back home, I remember standing next to this guy with his hands raised singing praises to God during worship. "Who is this person? What is my role now?" When we got home, I collapsed in bed and sobbed in fear of who I was not, fear of who I was becoming and confusion about who this new person was, I was still married to was now. God had taken this broken, beat up life of my husband's and made him new. I was left to watch and wonder in attempts to figure out where I fit into this new renewed life. It took me a long time and counsel to figure out who I was in Christ again.

A few months post confession, Tim was given a revelation though a mentor that really explained all my new fears. His selfish addictions stripped me of who I was over the years, and in doing so killed the very person he married, depleting so much of what I worked for. The devil knew this would become my weak spot and I have to fight against the urge to believe in his lies daily. This goes beyond the title of wife, mom, or co-worker. There are days where it takes me five outfits to finally decide on the one okay outfit to leave the house. My eyes for years saw a worthless, unqualified and not-good enough person to those I offered relationship to.

God continues to speak truth to me and squashes out the lies I believed about myself. Being in God's Word has been the biggest defense against the sin consequence of my mind.

Questions for Discussion and Reflection:

- How do you think people view you? If you had to write on a note card attributes about yourself, what would they be? Would they look different if you had your spouse write them or a close friend?

    LET'S PRACTICE!

- Where or what do you find your identity rooted in?

- What evidence is there that Christ is working in your life?

- Do your words match your actions? Is your faith visible to those around you?

What Does the Bible Say?

- **2 Corinthians 5:17,** "Therefore, if anyone is in Christ, he is a new creation; the old has gone, the new has come!"

- **Romans 8:1,** "Therefore, there is now no condemnation for those who are in Christ Jesus."

- **1 Peter 2:9,** "But you are a chosen people, a royal priesthood, a holy nation, a people belonging to God, that you may declare the praises of Him who called you out of darkness into his wonderful light."

- **John 15:5,** "I am the vine; you are the branches. If a man remains in me and I in him, he will bear much fruit; apart from me you can do nothing."

- **Philippians 3:20,** "But our citizenship is in heaven. And we eagerly await a Savior from there, the Lord Jesus Christ."

- **2 Timothy 1:7,** "For God did not give us a spirit of timidity, but a spirit of power, of love and of self-discipline."

- **Colossians 1:13-14,** "For he has rescued us from the dominion of darkness and brought us into the kingdom of the Son he loves, in whom we have redemption, the forgiveness of sins."

"God hath given you one face, and you make yourself another."

-William Shakespeare, Hamlet

Forgiveness

"When a deep injury is done to us, we never heal until we forgive."
- Nelson Mandela

God didn't wait to be crucified until we fully understood the impact His death would have on us. He _____. He _____. He _____ us life. Luke 23:34 says, "Father forgive them, for they do not know what they are doing." We need to respond in the same way; challenging ourselves to look past the scars and sometimes bloody mess, to offer forgiveness to those who have hurt us the worst because God did the same for you and for me. We _____ to forgive as we have been forgiven.

Inter-human evils, those done against and to other people, are some of the hardest situations to overcome. Such evils can be the hardest to forgive when done between husbands and wives, children and parents, co-workers and friends. The pain of betrayal makes for a very crucible experience. Webster Dictionary defines crucible as; "a severe test; a place or situation in which concentrated forces interact to cause or influence change or development." Walking through such a test will undoubtedly change who you are. The behaviors and choices that got you to this point, whether they were your choices made or not, should influence how your life will look like in the future. You won't forget the situation that brought such pain, but you **do not** need to endlessly _____ what happened. Forgiveness is the puzzle piece that will begin that process.

*"**We need to forgive others so Satan cannot take advantage of us.** We are commanded to get rid of all bitterness in our lives. Forgiving yourself is accepting the truth that God has already forgiven you in Christ. Forgiveness is not forgetting. **Once you choose to forgive someone, then Christ can come and begin to heal you of your hurts.** But the healing cannot begin until you first forgive. Forgiveness is mainly a matter of obedience to God. God wants you to be free; there is no other way. Don't wait until you feel like forgiving, You will never get there. Make the hard choice to forgive even if you don't feel like it. **Once you choose to forgive, Satan will have lost his power over you in that area, and God's healing touch will be free to move.**"*

Neil T. Anderson
The Bondage Breaker [9]

Over time, there are purposeful intentions that come out of the fire of evil. God is in this with us and up to something good.

What is forgiveness?

- Forgiveness is not letting the betrayer off the hook. We can, and should, still hold each other accountable for our actions, or lack of actions, in love as Christ did for us.

- Forgiveness is returning to God the right to take care of justice. It's not our job to punish people for their sins.

- Forgiveness does not mean we have to revert to being the victim. Forgiveness is an attitude.

- Forgiveness is not the same as reconciling. We can forgive someone even if we never can get along with him again. Forgiveness benefits the one offering it more than the one receiving it.

- If they don't repent, we still have to forgive. Even if they never ask, we need to forgive. We should memorize and repeat over and over: Forgiveness is about **our** attitude, not their action.

- Living with unforgiveness is like drinking the poison thinking the other person is going to die.

"A betrayer's humble repentance in word and deed will pave the way for the betrayed to again risk opening his or her heart and offering the sweet fruit of forgiveness that can lead to restoration and renewed joy."

- Tim Jackson

Questions for Discussion and Reflection:

- Are there areas in your life where forgiveness is needed?

- What is your attitude towards God when given the choice to forgive the one who hurt you? Do you feel like you rise above it and allow the good consequence to shine or find justice in the bitterness having sarcasm, anger and stewing rage be the fruit you produce? Do you feel challenged when God tells you to forgive?

What Does the Bible Say?

- **Ephesians 4:31-32,** "Get rid of all bitterness, rage and anger, brawling and slander, along with every form of malice. Be kind and compassionate to one another, forgiving each other, just as in Christ God forgave you."

- **Luke 6:37,** "Do not judge, and you will not be judged. Do not condemn, and you will not be condemned. Forgive, and you will be forgiven."

- **Mark 11:25,** "And when you stand praying, if you hold anything against anyone, forgive him, so that your Father in heaven may forgive you your sins."

- **Matthew 6:15,** "But if you do not forgive men their sins, your Father will not forgive your sins."

- **James 5:16,** "Therefore confess your sins to each other and pray for each other so that you may be healed. The prayer of a righteous man is powerful and effective."

- **Acts 2:38,** "Peter replied, "Repent and be baptized, every one of you, in the name of Jesus Christ for the forgiveness of your sins. And you will receive the gift of the Holy Spirit."

- **Gen. 50:17-21,** "This is what you are to say to Joseph: I ask you to forgive your brothers the sins and the wrongs they committed in treating you so badly.' Now please forgive the sins of the servants of the God of your father." When their message came to him, Joseph wept. His brothers then came and threw themselves down before him. "We are your slaves," they said. But Joseph said to them, "Don't be afraid. Am I in the place of God? You intended to harm me, but God intended it for good to accomplish what is now being done, the saving of many lives. So then, don't be afraid. I will provide for you and your children." And he reassured them and spoke kindly to them."

- **Numbers 14:20,** "The Lord replied, "I have forgiven them, as you asked."

- **Micah 7:18,** "Who is a God like you, who pardons sin and forgives the transgression of the remnant of his inheritance? You do not stay angry forever but delight to show mercy."

There is no reason to forgive unless you believe in something bigger than yourself.

"To be a Christian means to forgive the inexcusable because
Christ has forgiven the inexcusable in us."
- C.S.Lewis

Hope

"The way we go after opportunities reveals what we're made of.
The dew of blessing; the critical part of a Christian's gaze recognizing the blessings and goodness in a situation that also function to reveal the human heart."
- David Powlison

I wish hope was found as easily as dust bunnies quickly cluster together. Somedays it may feel like you need to tear down the walls of Jericho in order to see just a glimmer of hope shine through to your soul and other days it may shine through so brightly, like a clear sunny afternoon. It's in the moments where the sun is shining through and you sense progress and see hope, that you also see the dirt and smudges from the stresses of life too. Hope is not an emotion; it's an _____. We have to actively work on seeing the _____ in our situations and seeing God in the little moments weaving everything together for His _____ and His plan. Emotions can derail us from the progress much like the dirt and smudges on the windows allowing our vision to be clouded and blurred. God wants us to not see the stains, but instead the rays of hope shining through.

The fragrance of Christ appears in the context of having been sinned against, and is seen as mercy, forgiveness, courage, endurance, and the ability to **persevere in hope**.

Questions for Discussion and Reflection:

- What has hope looked like to you? Was it a person, a book, a rainbow, or something physical like a brush of a shoulder that indicated the road was turning upwards?

- Has it been hard to see through the smudges on the window? What do you do when you lose focus?

It's okay to have a healthy fear of starting over again.

"To love means loving the unlovable. To forgive means pardoning the unpardonable. Faith means believing the unbelievable. Hope means hoping when everything seems hopeless."
- G.K. Chesterton

What Does the Bible Say?

- **Job 5:16,** "So the poor have hope, and injustice shuts its mouth."

- **Psalm 9:18,** "But God will never forget the needy; the hope of the afflicted will never perish."

- **Psalm 33:22,** "May your unfailing love be with us, Lord, even as we put our hope in You."

- **Jeremiah 17:7,** "But blessed is the one who trusts in the Lord, whose confidence is in Him."

- **Joel 3:16,** "The Lord will roar from Zion and thunder from Jerusalem; the earth and the heavens will tremble. But the Lord will be a refuge for His people, a stronghold for the people of Israel."

- **Lamentations 3:25-26,** "The Lord is good to those whose hope is in Him, to the one who seeks Him; it is good to wait quietly for the salvation of the Lord."

- **Jeremiah 29:11,** "For I know the plans I have for you," declares the Lord, "plans to prosper you and not to harm you, plans to give you hope and a future."

Hope is God taking the impossible and giving you the strength to believe in the possible. I hope for my children to find Godly men and women to marry someday as they embark on this adult relationship stuff. I hope for Christ to come and save me from more pain before I experience it.

Hope is real. Hope is within our reach and God wants us to hope with great excitement in His expectation. It's what gets us to take that first step towards forgiveness, reconciliation, and sometimes that first hug we crave so intensely. Hope is part of a believers DNA and let us not forget it when life is completely out of control. "I wait for the Lord, my soul waits, and in His word I put my hope." **Psalm 130:5**

Further Questions for Discussion and Reflection:
- Is your hope in God? Do you believe He will overcome your pain?

In the dark dreary nights, when the storm is at its most fierce, the lighthouse burns bright so the sailors can find their way home again. In life the same light burns. This light is fueled with love, faith, and hope. And through life's most fierce storms these three burn their brightest so we also can find our way home again.

-Unknown

Additional Bible Verses

- **Psalm 62:5,** "Find rest, O my soul, in God alone; my hope comes from Him."

- **John 16:33,** "I have told you these things, so that in me you may have peace. In this world you will have trouble. But take heart! I have overcome the world."

- **Romans 8:18,** "I consider that our present sufferings are not worth comparing with the glory that will be revealed in us. The creation waits in eager expectation for the sons of God to be revealed."

- **Matthew 19:26,** "Jesus looked at them and said, "with man this is impossible, but with God, all things are possible."

- **Romans 5:3-5,** "Not only so, but we also rejoice in our sufferings, because we know that suffering produces perseverance, character; and character, hope. And hope does not disappoint us, because God has poured out His love into our hearts, by the Holy Spirit, whom He has given us."

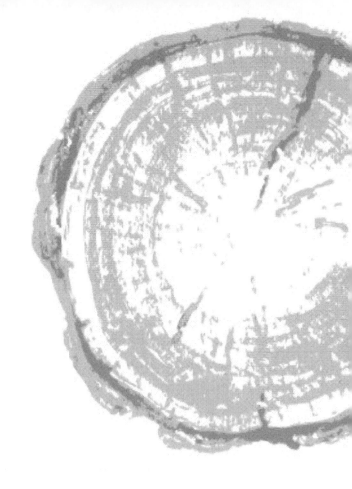

Trust

"Can trust be reborn? Yes, if integrity is reborn. Trust dies when integrity dies."
Gary Chapman

Trusting God after a painful betrayal in your marriage is like standing on a cliff near the Grand Canyon as God says, "I've got this. Trust me and I will _____ you, guide you, and give you what you need in this desperate time of suffering and anguish." Getting to the point where you can fall; eyes upward and heart in His hands; knowing all you need is to trust and obey, is so much easier said than done but _____ in your process to healing. (Please no cliff jumping. That's not what I'm encouraging!) When all is resolved and we reflect and see that God ultimately had our back, and our life was taken care of, it's easier to trust Him the next time we are faced with difficult circumstances. The same is true for our marriages. Trusting a spouse after betrayal takes a repetitive behavioral pattern of honesty and transparency, allowing the betrayed into choices that prove the betrayer is again worthy of trust.

Life experiences can make it hard to trust others with our hearts. I've been hurt by some of my closest friends and family members. It has made me cautious as to whom I share life with and whom I offer deep friendship to. BUT, God has never wavered and we can always run to Him, even when it is scary. Placing trust and hope in God means allowing Him to take you places you've never been before; to put you in uncomfortable situations which will result in experiencing His love in ways never thought possible. Often that means pausing mid-journey to reflect on the beauty in the pain, and to remind yourself that you can trust in Him as His will is perfected in your situation. And so goes the hymn...

"Trust and obey, for there's no other way
To be happy in Jesus, but to trust and obey.

When we walk with the Lord in the light of His Word,
What a glory He sheds on our way!
While we do His good will, He abides with us still,
And with all who will trust and obey.

Not a shadow can rise, not a cloud in the skies,
But His smile quickly drives it away;
Not a doubt or a fear, not a sigh or a tear,
Can abide while we trust and obey.

Not a burden we bear, not a sorrow we share,

But our toil He doth richly repay;

Not a grief or a loss, not a frown or a cross,

But is blessed if we trust and obey.

But we never can prove the delights of His love

Until all on the altar we lay;

For the favor He shows, for the joy He bestows,

Are for them who will trust and obey.

Then in fellowship sweet we will sit at His feet.

Or we'll walk by His side in the way.

What He says we will do, where He sends we will go;

Never fear, only trust and obey. [10]

Questions for Discussion and Reflection:

- Have there been situations in your life that have caused you to not trust others and your spouse completely?

- Do you give others close to you reasons to trust you and do you allow transparency within your marriage?

- If God threw you in the lions den, is your faith strong enough to trust in the promise of the Word knowing that God is with you?

What Does the Bible Say?

- **Proverbs 3:5,** "Trust in the Lord with all your heart, and lean not on your own understanding."

- **Jeremiah 17:7,** "But blessed is the man who trusts in the Lord, whose confidence is in Him."

- **Psalm 56:3,** "When I am afraid, I will trust in You."

- **Daniel 6:23**, "The king was overjoyed and gave orders to lift Daniel out of the den. And when Daniel was lifted from the Den, no wound was found on him, because he had trusted in his God."

- **Joshua 1:9**, "Have I not commanded you? Be strong and courageous. Do not be terrified; do not be discouraged. For the Lord your God will be with you wherever you go."

- **Isaiah 41:10**, "So do not fear, for I am with you; do not be dismayed, for I am your God. I will strengthen you and help you; I will uphold you with my righteous right hand."

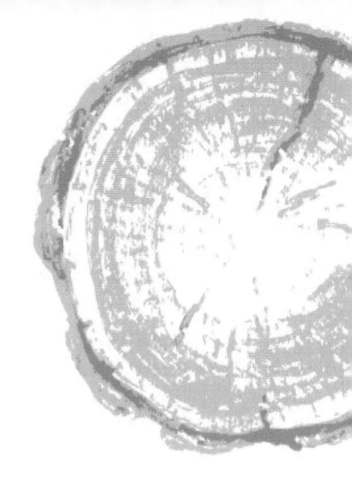

Education

Understanding the grip the enemy has over our minds and everyday life is crucial to protecting our marriages. "Covenant Eyes," is an internet accountability and filtering program which states these facts about the suffocating addiction of pornography:

75% of pastors do not make themselves accountable to anyone.

37% of pastors said viewing pornography was a "current struggle."[11]

81 million daily average visits to Pornhub, the world's most popular porn website.[12]

$20 billion annually is profited/generated globally from the pornography industry.[13]

1 in 5 mobile searches are for pornography.[14]

Some marriages today have a lack of understanding and never give thought to furthering their marital education. We get our college degree, exchange our "I do's", and then relish in the newlywed state of marriage for a few years, sometimes less. Then life happens, children appear, jobs overwhelm, and we are overtaken by daily routines mixed with household chores and driving kids from sports to school. How is it that we put thousands of dollars into a piece of paper that possibly will gain us a career and most often requires continued education, but we can't seem to prioritize the continuing education required for our marriage? It happens so slowly that we don't see it coming, but married life becomes something of "college _____" passing in the halls. We loose the ZEST in our relationship.

Part of our continued marriage education should be installing "_____" in our daily routines to guard against "_____" that mess with our thought process, make us stumble and lose our focus on the prize. Kids, ages 6-8, are being exposed for the first time to pornography. A stick of gum is being marketed with sex. Walking through a mall is eye candy to any weak mind that seeks lust before God. We have become numb to what we expose ourselves to and need to take back control within our marriage and home to what is first in our lives; Jesus.

It is imperative to know the "why" behind the confession or discovery. If you don't know what is broken, you don't know what to fix. Once you locate the cause, the catalyst to the confession, then you can install protective measures to guard against further fatal discoveries. This may mean you need to pull back layers, past years possibly back to your childhood, to resolve your why.

Questions for Discussion and Reflection:
- Is there a lack of "continued education" within your marriage?

- Are you intimidated by marriage conferences? Why? What would you want to see offered with regard to conferences/aids to marriages?

- Do you fear knowing more about your vows or do you trust God to reveal a deeper knowledge within your marriage commitment to each other?

- What are some ways that you have grown deeper in your marriage?

- What are some other ways we can guard ourselves, educate our marriages, and show others our respect for our spouses when in public?

Suggested websites to educate and protect:

www.covenanteyes.net

www.integrityrestored.com

www.qustodio.com

www.fightthenewdrug.org

www.netnanny.com

www.IMDb.com

Some men find a telephone pole attractive, so living like a cave man is not an option. It is through healthy boundaries and education as a couple, that can defeat the mind.

"For the word of God is living and active. Sharper than any double-edge sword, it penetrates even to dividing soul and spirit, joints and marrow; it judges the thoughts and attitudes of the heart."
Hebrews 4:12

What Does the Bible Say?

- **Proverbs 1:5,** "Let the wise listen and add to their learning, and let the discerning get guidance."

- **Proverbs 9:9,** "Instruct a wise man and he will be wiser still; teach a righteous man and he will add to his learning."

- **Proverbs 18:15,** "The heart of the discerning requires knowledge; the ears of the wise seek it out."

- **Ephesians 1:17,** "I keep asking that the God of our Lord Jesus Christ, the glorious Father, will give you the Spirit of wisdom and revelation, so that you may know Him better."

- **Colossians 1:9,** "For this reason, since the day we heard about you, we have not stopped praying for you and asking God to fill you with the knowledge of His will, through all spiritual wisdom and understanding."

Communication

Being able to have _____ communication in your relationship and finding new ways to _____ your love towards each other will not only build trust, but strengthen your vows. Gary Chapman in his book, *The Five Love Languages*, helps us discover what our love languages are and how vital it is to speak each others language in a marriage.

Allow your tone of voice, body language, and ability to speak in love, expand your relationship to the next level as you both _____ your new marriage. Sometimes that means going outside your comfort zone and having to discuss what you're REALLY thinking. This is hard, but trust me, the more honest and vulnerable you can be, generally will inspire the other to open up and meet you with the same vulnerability.

This may take a pile of humility on your part to sit and listen, but allow God to quiet you or quiet your spouse so you can really hear each others heart. Maybe start out simple by asking how the day was, or dive in and compliment your spouse with one reason why you appreciate them. This may be challenging if you are in a position of separation or divorce. Don't let that stop you. You have little eyes around you that are watching how you respond to this conflict. It's your choice to let the bad fruit spew out or the good fruit shine. (refer to the three tree diagram)

Questions for Discussion and Reflection:

- Do you sometimes feel like you're the only one who understands what is coming out of your mouth?

4 Common Responses That Can Ruin Relationships:

1. **Fight:** You attack others when you feel fearful; intimidating the other people; you have unreasonable demands that try to control the situation.
2. **Flight:** You find yourself busy with distractions; sleeping, hyper-activity, always gone doing things, never home, binge on Netflix.
3. **Freeze:** You give-up, blank-out, feel stuck, and hold breath in dread; dissociation, escapism.
4. **Fawn:** You tend to be a people pleaser; constantly walking on egg shells. You rarely show the real you to those around you.

- Which is your most common coping mechanism when feeling fearful, insecure or threatened?

- How is that coping mechanism affecting your marriage or other relationships?

- How has your body language changed the tone of conversation with others, and with your spouse?

- When discussing the raw heart issues in your marriage, do you find yourself speaking in humility and love, or anger and bitterness?

What Does the Bible Say?

- **Ephesians 4:29,** "Do not let any unwholesome talk come out of your mouths, but only what is helpful for building others up according to their needs, that it may benefit those who listen."

- **Hebrews 4:12,** "For the word of God is alive and active. Sharper than any doubled-edged sword, it penetrates even to dividing soul and spirit, joints and marrow; it judges the thoughts and attitudes of the heart."

- **James 1:19,** "Everyone should be quick to listen, slow to speak, and slow to become angry."

- **Psalm 19:14,** "May the words of my mouth and the meditation of my heart be pleasing in your sight, O Lord, my Rock and my Redeemer."

- **Proverbs 15:1,** "A gentle answer turns away wrath, but a harsh word stirs up anger."

- **Proverbs 12:18,** "Reckless words pierce like a sword, but the tongue of the wise brings healing."

- **Proverbs 16:24,** "Pleasant words are a honeycomb, sweet to the soul and healing to the bones."

Support

Do you remember playing the childhood game "Telephone"? You sit in a circle and start by whispering in one person's ear a statement and by the time it reaches the other end, the statement is twisted, backwards, and nowhere near the statement first spoken. It can be hilarious to see how fast the story can change and be altered simply because people aren't listening intently or are in a rush and say something backwards. Same goes for when you say something in confidence to a friend or in passing to someone that asks, "How are you doing?" It always amazes me how quickly stories can be changed for the worse if not protected.

I was once told to protect my story as it was mine to share when I felt compelled to share and when I felt safe enough to bring light to my marital situation. For years after Tim and I went through our dark valley, just our immediate family, pastors, and two close friends knew the struggles we were dealing with. I had a few clients who knew, but it was only because of tears, or having to reschedule appointments, that they found out. We knew that in order to fix us we had to protect our journey by keeping silence so outside opinions and games of "telephone" didn't work against our progress. We surrounded our little family with those that would uplift us, pray for us and stand behind us in the trenches. Anything outside of that would have just been noise, and a distraction from the hard work we needed to complete.

Jesus did the same as He performed miracles when walking on this earth. Jesus had His 12 disciples come alongside Him to pray for Him, support Him, and set the story straight when whispers started to spread.

Questions for Discussion and Reflection:
- Are you taking measures to protect YOUR story?

- Have you been supportive & respectful of your spouse when sharing your story?

What Does the Bible Say?

- **Acts 15:32**, "Judas and Silas, who themselves were prophets, said much to encourage and strengthen the believers."

- **Romans 15:7**, "Accept one another, then, just as Christ accepted you, in order to bring praise to God."

- **Hebrews 10:24,** "And let us consider how we may spur one another on toward love and good deeds."

- **Galatians 6:2,** "Carry each other's burdens, and in this way you will fulfill the law of Christ."

- **Romans 12:11,13,** "Never be lacking in zeal, but keep your spiritual fervor, serving the Lord... Share with the Lord's people who are in need. Practice hospitality."

Restoration: building blocks

The Vinedresser does not start with the clippers; He starts with the snips.

"Love is an art to be learned and a discipline to be maintained."
- Ed Wheat

"I am the vine; you are the branches. If a man remains in me and I in him, he will bear much fruit; apart from me you can do nothing. My command is this: Love each other as I have loved you. Greater love has no one than this, that he lay down his life for his friends."
John 15:5,12-13

Building a new marriage means you "create the sacred" in the marriage again. You must learn to cherish your spouse and be transparent with each other.

In Biblical times, people grew a hedge of thorns around their gardens and even their houses as a method of protection. Likewise, we need to build a hedge of protection around our marriages. Job 1:10 says, "Have you not put a hedge around him and his household and everything he has? You have blessed the work of his hands, so that his flocks and herds are spread throughout the land."

We must agree to not take any chances with our marriage when trying to protect and restore what was broken. Aspects of the hedge can be found in education, through proper support and counsel, ultimately in cementing your faith in the One who can restore even the ugliest of sins.

Nothing lasting happens overnight. It takes time, God will reward you for the decision to choose restoration, and He will grant you the patience needed as you make mistakes and work together to change. God will not judge and wants us to follow His example when we confess to one another and seek transparency in our relationships. You might not see progress when comparing to the day before, but over time, with God's help, you will see a beautifully restored and renewed marriage.

The restoration and purification of your heart and marriage is one of the prime works of the Holy Spirit. He (God) will shake you loose, set you free and grant you patience for the process. Remember the process gold must go through to get to its pure state. It must endure the fire to burn off the rubbish or it will always just be a dull, shapeless lump. It is in the process of going through the fire that all the not-so-glorious parts are burned off to allow the perfect and beautiful parts to shine brightly.

Questions for Discussion and Reflection:

- How has God given you patience to mend and restore what was broken?

- Do you feel you have the tools necessary to remodel your relationship? If not, have you found the courage to speak up and ask for help?

"You don't have the luxury of planning even the next sentence to come out of your mouth. You immediately publish the distempers or radiancies of your soul. You publish by the questions you ask (or don't ask), by how you listen (or don't really want to listen), by the interpretations you offer (or don't even think to offer), by the advice you give (or can't give), by the attitude you take towards people, towards problems and towards people with problems."
- David Powlison

- Locating your current struggles, and identifying what they mean, allows you to see what exactly is at stake and where you are going. Are you able to locate your situation (the heat) and see the difference between truth and lies? The restoration process can only begin when you allow God to start pruning your own heart.

- What are some ways that you have restored your marriage and God has healed your heart? If the marriage dissolved in a divorce, have you been able to see restoration within other relationships that surrounded your marriage?

Remember a small start can lead to big change!

What Does the Bible Say?

- **Psalm 91 - The Prayer of Protection:** Whoever dwells in the shelter of the Most High will rest in the shadow of the Almighty. I will say of the Lord, "He is my refuge and my fortress, my God, in whom I trust." Surely he will save you from the fowler's snare and from the deadly pestilence. He will cover you with his feathers, and under his wings you will find refuge; his faithfulness will be your shield and rampart. You will not fear the terror of night, nor the arrow that flies by day, nor the pestilence that stalks in the darkness, nor the plague that destroys at midday. A thousand may fall at your side, ten thousand at your right hand, but it will not come near you. You will only observe with your eyes and see the punishment of the wicked. If you say, "The Lord is my refuge," and you make the Most

High your dwelling, no harm will overtake you, no disaster will come near your tent. For he will command his angels concerning you to guard you in all your ways; they will lift you up in their hands, so that you will not strike your foot against a stone. You will tread on the lion and the cobra; you will trample the great lion and the serpent.

"Because he loves me," says the Lord, "I will rescue him; I will protect him, for he acknowledges my name. He will call on me, and I will answer him; I will be with him in trouble, I will deliver him and honor him. With long life I will satisfy him and show him my salvation."

- **Psalm 23:3,** "He refreshes my soul, He guides me along the right paths for His name's sake."

- **Psalm 51:12,** "Restore to me the joy of your salvation and grant me a willing spirit, to sustain me."

- **Ecclesiastes 4:12,** "Though one may be overpowered, two can defend themselves. A cord of three strands is not quickly broken."

- **Jeremiah 30:17,** "But I will restore you to health and heal your wounds, declares the Lord"

- **Joel 2:26,** "You will have plenty to eat, until you are full, and you will praise the name of the Lord your God, who has worked wonders for you; never again will my people be shamed."

- **Revelations 21:1-5,** "Then I saw "a new heaven and a new earth," for the first heaven and the first earth had passed away, and there was no longer any sea. I saw the Holy City, the new Jerusalem, coming down out of heaven from God, prepared as a bride beautifully dressed for her husband. And I heard a loud voice from the throne saying, "Look! God's dwelling place is now among the people, and he will dwell with them. They will be his people, and God himself will be with them and be their God. 'He will wipe every tear from their eyes. There will be no more death' or mourning or crying or pain, for the old order of things has passed away."

- **Romans 5:9-10,** "Since we have now been justified by his blood, how much more shall we be saved from God's wrath through him."

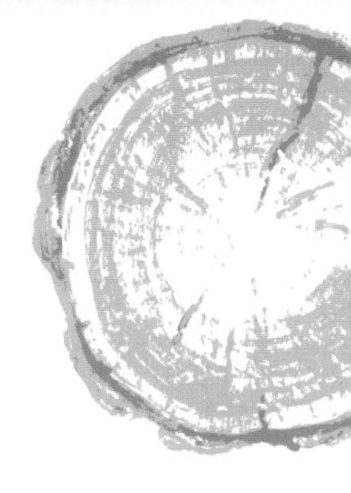

Redeemed

"The measure of Christ's glory is the difference between what you would be by nature, and what you are because of Christ."

- Jack Miller

We have been purchased!!

It happened when Jesus took our sins upon the wooden cross in His death and resurrection, an exchange for the freedom to live. Forever redeemed. Forever saved from this ugly, fallen world we live in. Three nails and our lives are completely changed. Ever think about what life would be like without the gift of forgiveness and grace? A life without redemption is a life captured in slavery. Christ's blood freed us from the bondage of sin; the cross released us physically from the torment of slavery (our sins) in order to have the ability to reproduce good fruit (works) to glorify Him.

God has a funny way of using our deepest wounds to show His glory to others but more importantly, to show us where our character lacked strength. How has God reconstructed your character and given you redemption through the pain?

Questions for Discussion and Reflection:

- What is the meaning of redemption? What does the Bible say about it?

What Does the Bible Say?

- **Psalm 111:9,** "How can a young person stay on the path of purity? By living according to your word."

- **Galatians 2:20,** "I have been crucified with Christ and I no longer live, but Christ lives in me. The life I now live in the body, I live by faith in the Son of God, who loved me and gave himself for me."

- **Colossians 1:13-14,** "For he has rescued us from the dominion of darkness and brought us into the kingdom of the Son he loves, in whom we have redemption, the forgiveness of sins."

- **Psalm 19:14,** "May these words of my mouth and the meditation of my heart, be pleasing in your sight, Lord, my Rock, and my Redeemer."

- **Hebrews 9:14,** "How much more, then, will the blood of Christ, who through the eternal Spirit offered himself unblemished to God, cleanse our consciences from acts that lead to death, so that we may serve the living God!"

- **Revelations 5:12,** " Worthy is the Lamb, who was slain, to receive power and wealth and wisdom and strength and honor and glory and praise!"

- **Titus 2:14**, "Who gave himself for us to redeem us from all wickedness and to purify for himself a people that are his very own, eager to do what is good."

- **Ephesians 1:7,** "In him we have redemption through his blood, the forgiveness of sins, in accordance with the riches of God's grace that he lavished on us with all wisdom and understanding."

"Redeemed women of God have tender merciful hearts, backbones of steel, and hands that are prepared for the fight." - Stasi Eldredge

Joy: choosing to see

When our lives are _____ with God's Word, we should be experiencing _____ everyday, in many ways. God challenges us to _____ _____ in our trials because He knows that it will build _____ and make us _____. We have to work to find it, though, and that requires action!

Over the years, I have seen the devil rip marriages apart and cause dissension in the church from the temptations of the world and consequences that follow. I've witnessed people choosing bitterness instead of forgiveness, and then realizing that the grass is not greener on the other side. I've seen a well of emotions reappear after 35 years of betrayal and the pain, caused by the lack of grace given. Generations suffer from selfish decisions and buried joy because facing the truth is just too hard. The devil is having a party as he brings chaos to our marriages and casts a sky of despair over those too weak to fight the battle.

In the Old Testament we see that joy was associated with true worship of God. During King Hezekiah's reign, the Israelites rededicated themselves to God and we read that the people renewed their commitment to God which ultimately reignited the joy in their hearts. Paul experienced joy by simply doing God's will in his ministry and encourages us to find joy in Christ's sufferings. James tells us to "count it all joy" when we are facing trials or in the midst of suffering. The only thing that can steal our joy is sin. By encompassing your life with His Word and His truth, you protect yourself against the flaming arrows that want to rip away your hard earned smile, destroy the baby steps made towards your healing, and reduce the joy that is promised to you through Christ. Allow the joy to shine through to the outside and let others see the beauty in the ashes as God restores your heart and heals your wounds.

Questions for Discussion and Reflection:

- In Isaiah 55:12, we are told to "go out with joy and be led forth in peace." Have you been able to follow through with that command as you face personal struggles and hardships?

- What things bring you joy from sunrise to sunset?

What does the Bible say?

- **Ecclesiastes 7:14,** "When times are good, be happy; but when times are bad, consider: God has made the one as well as the other."

- **Philippians 4:4-7,** "Rejoice in the Lord always, I will say it again: Rejoice! Let your gentleness be evident to all. The Lord is near. Do not be anxious about anything, but in everything by prayer and petition, with thanksgiving, present your requests to God. And the peace of God, which transcends all understanding, will guard your hearts and your minds in Christ Jesus."

- **Romans 12:12,** "Be joyful in hope, patient in affliction, faithful in prayer."

- **James 1:2-3,** "Consider it pure joy, my brothers and sisters, whenever you face trials of many kinds, because you know that the testing of your faith produces perseverance."

- **Galatians 5:22,** "But the fruit of the Spirit is love, joy, peace, forbearance, kindness, goodness, faithfulness, gentleness, and self control."

- **Psalm 16:9,** "Therefore my heart is glad and my tongue rejoices; my body will also rest secure."

- **Psalm 71:23,** "My lips will shout for joy, when I sing praise to you - I whom you have delivered."

- **Psalm 126:5,** "Those who sow with tears, will reap with songs of joy."

"Fear & doubt are conquered by a faith that rejoices. And faith can rejoice because the promises of God are as certain as God Himself."

-Kay Arthur

Boundaries: we all need them

"I once heard that the Greek term for "weaker partner" can also be translated "fine china," which I think is a better translation within the context of marriage. How do you handle fine china? With respect, as you tenderly appreciate and display its finest points. You don't slam fine china around or put it through the blast of a dishwasher."

Fred & Brenda Stoeker

Every Heart Restored[15]

Boundaries are not meant to be boring, make you feel boxed in or caged, or even meant to isolate you from those in your daily life. Boundaries are meant to protect, guide and give others a gauge of what, where and who you are willing to enjoy life with. If we don't have any boundaries, we allow ourselves to be tossed around and become hurt in the process.

Communicating our boundaries with our loved ones is vital to the success of our relationships. Telling those closest to you "that's not okay," or "I'm not going there as it will cause me to stumble," is key to later conversations and consequences. In marriages, having healthy boundaries is like taking a daily vitamin to keep your body strong and in balance. Just like we handle fine china, we need to handle our relationships with care. Some of us may need more boundaries than others; THAT'S OKAY!

If you come from a background where pornography plagues your mind, you shouldn't be going to a movie, dinner or event that would challenge your eyes and mind. Many couples find staying away from alcohol as a boundary they're not willing to budge on in their home or when out with friends. Some have boundaries with their kids that may differ from other parents, and most of us have those in place due to our childhood. As believers, we have a set of boundaries laid out for us in the Bible that can help us determine what is healthy and what is not as we overcome challenges, fears, and betrayal in our lives. Everyone's WILL look different but are necessary to succeed.

Questions for Discussion and Reflection:

- Do you find it hard to place boundaries in your life and stick to them? Did you have clear boundaries prior to the betrayal in your marriage?

- Does your spouse agree to the need to establish boundaries around the areas that caused the betrayal to happen?

- Has it been hard to deal with someone who may appear like "fine china"?

What does the Bible Say?

- **Matthew 4:6-7,** "If you are the Son of God," he said, "throw yourself down. For it is written: "He will command his angels concerning you, and they will lift you up in their hands, so that you will not strike your foot against a stone."'

- **Isaiah 58:11,** "The Lord will guide you always; he will satisfy your needs in a sun scorched land and will strengthen your frame. You will be like a well-watered garden, like a spring whose waters never fail."

- **Matthew 5:37,** "All you need to say is simply 'Yes' or 'No'; anything beyond this comes from the evil one."

- **Luke 16:13,** "No one can serve two masters. Either you will hate the one and love the other, or you will be devoted to the one and despise the other. You cannot serve both God and money."

Perspective: Stubbed Toes

One morning as I was opening the blinds and turning the lights on, I clumsily stumbled into the LARGE table that had been sitting in the same place for years. It is beyond frustrating to stub your toe, and unbelievable how something so small can create such pain! I immediately had shooting pain and within an hour a black and purple pinkie toe. As I was icing my "serious" injury, I had an epiphany: Sometimes the pain we encounter due to a ridiculous injury like stubbing our toes, parallels how simple, avoidable sins can affect our daily lives. There are obvious places, triggers, and things in our society and everyday lives that we KNOW will cause pain, but we still run into them and stumble because as humans we are weak and far from perfect.

I love what Beth Moore says, "Measure the size of the obstacle against the size of God." How quickly are we to forget the size of God when placed in a difficult situation? We see the obstacles in front of us, feel the pain from the punches, and experience the emotional grief caused by the sinful actions. In the moment, we focus on the initial pain that has been caused and aren't capable to see past the hurt to the bigger picture of the situation. It's not until we take a step back, that we see how we might have been able to avoid the pain, or see how God was, and has been by our side through every side kick, jab, or punch that came our way.

Whether it be fighting a debilitating health issue, dealing with naughty children, frayed friendships, avoiding addictions, stubbing toes or trying to pick up the pieces of your marriage, let God change your perspective so you can see all the _____ in the _____.

Questions for Discussion and Reflection:

- Can you relate to the notecard exercise and if so, how much clarity do you have in your journey? How blurry is your "notecard?"

- Has God change your perspective on issues within your marriage?

- Have you been able to grow your character when you "stubbed" your toes?

What does the Bible say?

** I can't forgive myself and those who have hurt me.

- **1 John 1:9,** "If we confess our sins, He is faithful and just and will forgive us our sins and purify us from all unrighteousness."

- **Romans 8:1,** "Therefore, there is now no condemnation for those who are in Christ Jesus."

** I can't keep going. I'm tired.

- **Psalm 91:15,** "He will call on me, and I will answer Him; I will be with him in trouble, I will deliver him and honor him."

- **2 Corinthians 12:9,** "But He said to me, "My grace is sufficient for you, for my power is made perfect in weakness." Therefore I will boast all the more gladly about my weaknesses, so that Christ's power may rest on me."

** I feel so alone.

- **Hebrews 13:5,** "Keep your lives free from the love of money and be content with what you have, because God has said, "Never will I leave you; never will I forsake you."

- **Genesis 2:18,** "The Lord God said, "It is not good for the man to be alone. I will make a helper suitable for him."

** This is too hard to deal with.

- **Philippians 4:13,** "I can do all this through Him who gives me strength."

- **1 Peter 5:7,** "Cast all your anxiety on Him because He cares for you."

- **John 16:33,** "I have told you these things, so that in me you may have peace. In this world you will have trouble. But take heart! I have overcome the world."

** I'm afraid.

- **2 Timothy 1:7,** "For the Spirit God gave us does not make us timid, but gives us power, love and self discipline."

- **Psalm 23:4,** "Even though I walk through the darkest valley, I will fear no evil, for You are with me; Your rod and Your staff, they comfort me."

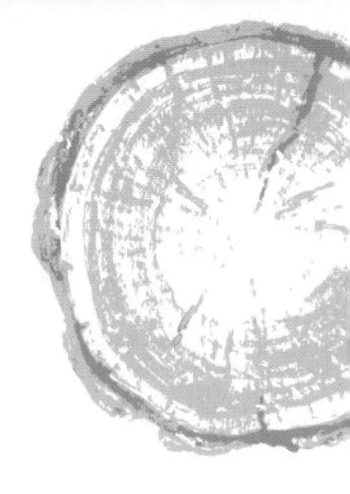

Dating: creating the new "us"

In the beginning of our time together, we talked about grieving over the death of your marriage. We've walked through the emotions of betrayal and discussed ways to protect against further confessions. It's almost impossible to not think about the person who sinned against us, but we've challenged each other to keep the focus on our own hearts. We've invited forgiveness into our lives as we seek more depth to our healing journeys, praying God would reveal the dark places in our lives that needed His mercy.

Now it's time to dance.

The dance you and your spouse were doing before led to destructive behaviors. Finding a new dance can be terrifying, exhausting and requires some level of trust that may not be existent yet. But, I want to encourage you to try! Start small and give yourself room to stumble.

Tim and I started dating each other again after the days of separation and beyond. At first it was all I could handle to just have him sitting on the couch across from me. That soon changed and we found ourselves at a coffee shop, then dinner. We had to start all over again, but it was worth every new move and twirl in our marriage to get to where we are today. Yes, there will be setbacks, discouraging conversations or painful counseling appointments you sit through, but the risk is worth the reward.

I can't promise you your marriage will end with happy ever afters. I can't promise you that there won't be more pain and struggle. God tells us in John 16:33 that, "In this world you will have trouble. But take heart! I have overcome the world." The purpose of this course was to reclaim our hearts back to God and to give Him all the glory for our story. If you find yourself in a place with a new sense of peace and clarity, a place where your identity and image is seen through the eyes of Christ, then our time together served it's purpose.

My husband and I are still working on our new dance moves. We don't get it right all the time, but there is a new desire and urgency to serve each other well through our marriage. Creating a new us has been filled with great rewards. If there was anything second to that, it would be the revelation in my own heart of how much my God loves me, cherishes me and wants His best for my life.

Its time for a new dance...what is it going to look like?

Date Night Ideas:
(think of this as self care activities)

• Go ice skating, roller skating, or play a round of miniature golf
• Go on a scavenger hunt

- Go to the park and swING!
- Find a worship service or concert to attend
- Find a coffee house and play board games
- Find a place to volunteer your time to bless others in need
- Take an exercise class together
- Look through old photo albums together
- Set a candle light dinner/picnic and have the kids be your waiters/waitresses
- Go on a photo date! Snap pictures around town then develop them to create a day date photo album
- Walk the mall. Goal is not to buy but to test perfume and cologne along the way
- Re-live a date before you were married starting with the first place you went out for dinner
- Steal the kids' toys and fly a kite!

Questions for Discussion and Reflection:

- What are some other encouraging, interactive date night ideas?

Suggested Book Resources

- Hope For The Separated *by Gary Chapman*
- The Bondage Breaker *by Neil T. Anderson*
- Every Heart Restored *by Fred & Brenda Stoeker*
- Every Man's Battle *by Steven Arterburn & Fred Stoeker*
- Every Woman's Battle *by Shannon Ethridge*
- Through A Man's Eyes *by Shaunti Feldhahn*
- Swipe Right *by Levi Lusko*
- Sex, Jesus, And the Conversations The Church Forgot *by Mo Isom*
- A Marriage Without Regrets *by Kay Arthur* (study guide available)
- How We Love *by Milan & Kay Yerkovich*
- The Five Love Languages *by Gary Chapman*
- Love & Respect *by Dr. Emerson Eggerichs* (study guide available)
- Desperate Marriages *by Gary Chapman*
- One More Try *by Gary Chapman*
- Sacred Marriage *by Gary Thomas*
- Boundaries In Marriage *by Henry Cloud & Dr. John Townsend*
- The Love Dare *by Alex Kendrick*
- Lies Women Believe *by Nancy Leigh DeMoss*
- Crazy Love *by Francis Chan*
- When His Secret Sin Breaks Your Heart *by Kathy Gallagher*
- Intimate Deception *by Dr. Sherri Keffer*
- Codependent No More *by Melody Beattie*
- Beauty Marks *by Linda Barriack*
- Men Are From Mars, Women Are From Venus *by John Gray*
- The Emotionally Destructive Marriage *by Leslie Vernick*
- Laugh Your Way To A Better Marriage *by Mark Gungor* (DVD series available)
- Broken & Redeemed: A Study On The God Who Redeems Our Stories *by A Love God Greatly Journal*

Online Resources

- Healing Hearts Ministry: The Hem of His Garment Bible Study www.healinghearts.org
- Marriage Teams: Empowering Couples for Winning Marriages www.marriageteam.org

Fill In the Blank Answer Key

Betrayal: weakest, rely, past, closer, heat

Bitterness: heat, consequences

Shame: decision, regret

Grief: permission,

    1. shock & denial

    2. pain & guilt, disappointment

    3. anger

    4. bargaining

    5. depression & sorrow

    6. testing & reconstruction

    7. acceptance

Weariness: acknowledge, strength, grace, you, you

Image: who you, individual, together, identity, consequences, found, Savior

Forgiveness: died, forgave, gave, need, revisit

Hope: verb, best, purpose

Trust: protect, necessary

Education: understanding, educated, roommates, installing firewalls, viruses

Communication: transparent, express, rediscover

Joy: in line, joy, find joy, character, stronger

Perspective: glory, story

Acknowledgements

Reclaimed Small Group Guide was birthed from a multitude of emotional coffee dates with broken women. Women who have experienced similar betrayal as myself and who continue to pursue healing. To God be all the glory in the many stories he continues to mold into greatness. For each hurting wife who trusted me with her story and allowed me to walk alongside her, I thank you.

Tim, my love and my husband. Without your confession, we would not be who we are today. Tim, thank you for your obedience to confess, your willingness to listen to God's voice, your choice to become accountable, and your steady love when I am unlovable. Thank you for loving me during my ugly moments and accepting the space needed to take back our marriage. Thank you for giving me full transparency into your heart and mind so that I could learn to trust and love you more than I ever thought possible. You and me, my love. You are the leader Jesus has always wanted for our family, and I'm truly honored to be your bride.

Pastor Kim and his wife Anne Ryan, thank you for being incredibly bold yet gentle mentors in our lives, both before and after the confession. Your grace and ability to speak truth into my life that first night changed the tone of my marriage.

Mom and Dad, thank you for never judging or pointing fingers when things all fell apart. Your sacrifice to love me unconditionally has been a remarkable example of Christ's love. I will forever appreciate all the moments you held me when weeping or gave me room to process as you graciously cared for our kids. I'm so grateful for your continued active role in their lives. You are my inspiration. I love you both so very much.

Catherine, my friend and sister in Christ, thank you for catching me minutes after Tim's confession, even with all the snot and tears of confusion falling to the floor. Your immediate willingness to hold my hand through such intense moments spoke to me of forgiveness and humility. Thank you for our times in search of God's beauty near your home and for encouraging me to build in self-care. Your prophetic word over my life continues to become reality. I am forever grateful for our friendship.

Pastor Kurt, the support and words of affirmation you have given toward our ministry and our marriage have been exceptionally powerful to both Tim and me. Your honesty, messages of truth and hope, and your friendship are never taken for granted.

Ramona and Michelle, thank you for your constant encouragement and gentle nudge to turn this study into a reality. Your support in the ministry has been unwavering.

And to all our other *family and friends*, thank you for your constant love and forgiveness toward me whether you knew my story or not. To those who cried with me, cheered me with countless hours of support, and prayed quietly when you knew I was weak, thank you.

Notes

1. Catherine Theriault, personal handwritten prayer, "A whisper from God," April 2009

2. J. Allan Peterson, The Myth of the Greener Grass(Tyndale House Publishers; 1984), 111.

3. Tim Jackson, When A Spouse Is Unfaithful, by Our Daily Bread®, © 1999, 2002 Our Daily Bread Ministries, Grand Rapids, MI. Reprinted by permission. All rights reserved.

4. Nelson's Compact Bible Commentary, 549.

5. Neil T. Anderson, The Bondage Breaker (Harvest House Publishers: 2006), 222-224.

6. Christian Jarrett, "Does This Brain Research Prove That Humiliation Is The Most Intense Human Emotion?" May 5 2014, https://www.wired.com/2014/05/does-this-brain-research-prove-that-humiliation-is-the-most-intense-human-emotion/.

7. https://www.crosswalk.com/faith/bible-study/the-most-frequent-command-in-the-bible.html

8. "Who we REALLY are - Our identity in Christ," GreatBibleStudy.com http://www.greatbiblestudy.com/who_we_really_are.php

9. Neil T. Anderson, The Bondage Breaker (Harvest House Publishers: 2006).

10. "Trust and Obey" lyrics by John H. Sammis (1846–1919), music by Daniel B. Towner (1850–1919); Public Domain

11. Leadership Journal, "Leadership Survey."

12. "The Most Viewed Porn Categories Of 2017 Are PRetty Messed Up." Fight the New Drug. https://fightthenewdrug.org/pornhub-reports-most-viewed-porn-of-2017/ (accessed May 21, 2018).

13. Paul M. Barret, "The new republic of porn," Bloomberg Businessweek, June 21, 2012.https://www.bloomberg.com/news/articles/2012-06-21/the-new-republic-of-porn (accessed June7, 2018).

14. Maryam Kamvar and Shumeet Baluja, "A large scale study of wireless search behavior: Google mobile search." CHI 06: Proceedings of the SIGCHI Conference on Human Factors in Computing Systems (2006): 701-709. http://www.kevinli.net/courses/mobilehci_w2012/papers/googlemobilesearch.pdf (accessed June 7, 2018).

15. Stephen Arterburn, Fred Stoeker, Brenda Stoeker, Every Heart Restored (WaterBrook press: 2004).

About the Author

Stephanie Broersma is a living example of how God brings beauty from ashes in the lives of His children. Married since 2002, she and her husband, Tim, have walked through the valley of marital betrayal and come out the other side stronger, more in love, and fully devoted to Christ. She now heads Reclaimed Ministry, an organization that seeks to help other broken brides recover from the pain and devastation of marital infidelity.

Visit **www.reclaimedministry.com** to watch the Broersma's testimony videos, and read more about the Reclaimed Ministry.

Photo credit by Jodi Van Straalen and the SNAPsisters Photography. www.thesnapsisters.com

Visit **www.reclaimedministry.com** for more information, to purchase *Reclaimed* products, and to see where a small group meets near you.

67853424R00046

Made in the USA
Columbia, SC
02 August 2019